30 PERFECT POPCORN
Recipes

How to Make Sweet & Savory
Gourmet Popcorn at Home

LORI JANE STEWART

Contents

Introduction

Popcorn has probably been around longer than any other snack food on the planet. It has a rich history, dating back to before civilization and taking part in a multitude of events we celebrate every year. It's the most popular snack food around the world, and the second most popular snack in America (falling just behind potato chips). Popcorn can be found all over the country, at movie theaters, carnivals, and most people's kitchens or pantries.

It is a common misconception that popcorn is an unhealthy snack. The reason some people avoid popcorn is because they don't understand the real culprit! Behind its supposedly unhealthy status, are the seasonings and additives, often added to commercially packaged products to liven up the bland natural flavor and to lengthen it's shelf life. The popcorn itself is a wholegrain, and these can help prevent cancer and lower the risk of heart disease, while also supplying healthy nutrients that support our vision.

There are many different methods to create popcorn, but the basic principle stays the same. All you have to do is make the kernels hot enough to heat the moisture contained naturally inside, and turn that into steam. The steam creates pressure from inside the hard shell casing and before you know it, POP!—the kernel is turned inside out and is ready to be consumed. As long as you can generate heat and have some kernels on hand, you can make popcorn!

Enough of the history, what about the recipes? I've gathered 30 of the finest popcorn recipes from around the world for your snacking pleasure, and have tried to keep them free from artificial sweeteners, preservatives or other nasty additives wherever possible. I've specified 9 cups of popped corn for most recipes, as that gives 3 generous cups per serving—you can have as many or as few servings as you fancy, but keep an eye on the calories! For your convenience, I've also included nutritional data from the USDA for each recipe—that's the U.S. Department of Agriculture and not the United Square Dancers of America!

My preference for both flavor and health reasons, is freshly air-popped popcorn—so I have used that kind for all of these recipes. Everything in this book can be made with kernels you have freshly popped, or if you are in a hurry (or feeling lazy!), then you can always use the plain store bought pre-popped variety—just make sure you check the packaging for artificial nasties!

Most of the ingredients for these recipes can be found at your local grocery store or deli, but if you get stuck, then the slightly more unusual ones can also be bought online via this special page on my website—www. greengourmetbooks.com/ing

Enjoy preparing and sharing!

Lori

P.S.—If 30 recipes isn't quite enough for you, then check the back of the book to find out how to get another 12, absolutely free!

Popcorn and Health

We live in a health conscious society with dietary obsessions intensifying each and every day. It sometimes feels like there are more diet programs, health "facts" and fat loss solutions than there are people in the world! Unfortunately, many of us are happy to accept any quick weight loss scam that comes along, often without doing any background research. And then we wonder why we have gained five pounds in five days—instead of losing the twenty pounds the new fad diet promised! You could write books longer than encyclopedia collections, just on all the common health misconceptions blasted at us on TV, in magazines and the good old, ever reliable internet, every day! We are going to ignore all of those, and instead focus on a food item that we encounter many times a year—and as you might have guessed, that's going to be popcorn!

Popcorn is the second most popular snack consumed by Americans; the first being potato chips. It is consumed in droves every day at movie theaters, amusement parks, carnivals, and thousands of homes. There are hundreds of different varieties of popcorn—salted, buttered, cinnamon glazed, and candy coated are just a few of the most common varieties that you can find on any grocery store's shelves. There has to be at least one flavor or popcorn variation available that for everyone will enjoy. But just how healthy is popcorn?

Before we pull out all the big chemistry words that you're going to take note of and forget in the next twenty minutes, let's take a look at this from a commonsense point of view. More than **three million** bags of microwave popcorn are sold each and every year in America, a country well known for having a large overweight and otherwise unhealthy population. If popcorn is the second most popular snack in a country full of overweight people, then it would be reasonable to assume that popcorn is fattening—right?

WRONG!

This is the exact same argument that is used by some people to condemn just about everything, other than tofu and vegan cheese. It is what many of us think when we deny ourselves a simple bag of popcorn, on the rare occasion we manage to see a movie at the theater. Moderation in most things is good, but a lot of the misconceptions about health and diet have caused millions of people to miss out on treats like popcorn, for no good reason whatsoever.

Plain air popped popcorn is healthy!

That's right, I said it, and I'm not taking it back either! Popcorn is a wholegrain. It's essentially just a heated up seed. Each kernel, by itself, contains very few calories or carbohydrates. It does not make you fat, and has little to do with the creation of fat in your body. Wholegrains are the healthiest grains you can consume, and have been linked to reducing the risk of diabetes and heart disease.

Let's get into the chemical aspects for a second. Popcorn has a large amount of polyphenols, an antioxidant that has been found to prevent cancer and reduce the risk of heart disease. Popcorn is also high in lutein and zeaxanthin, two chemicals commonly found in fruits and vegetables, that promote healthy vision and are known to reduce your risk of cataracts.

So, that means we can eat all the popcorn we want without consequence—right? While theoretically that may be correct, realistically it is a terrible idea. Plain popcorn is a simple wholegrain that you can snack on, worry-free. Unfortunately, popcorn by itself is pretty bland and boring. Adding salt, butter, and other ingredients is what gives popcorn it's appealing flavor, and it's these extras that are often bad for your health. By loading your popcorn down with butter, you're effectively making all its healthy properties insignificant.

Boring, plain and healthy in reasonable quantities, or exciting, delicious in smaller quantities—it's up to you!

To make the decision easier, I have made sure that all the recipes in this book have the nutritional information listed, calculated from the ingredients. So you can see at a glance which are most suited to your dietary requirements. The percent daily values are based on the Reference Daily Intake (RDI) for a 2000 calorie diet.

The History &
Popularity of Popcorn

*P*opcorn is one of the most common snacks eaten throughout the world. In the United States, it is the second most popular snack, just behind potato chips. Most of us have had popcorn at one point in time and have our own opinions on the timeless and cultureless snack, which has been revamped and reinvented countless times over its history.

Just how old is popcorn?

Archaeologists have found evidence that way back in eighty BC cavemen were eating maize, whose kernels could be heated up to create popcorn. There isn't sufficient evidence as to whether or not early man created and consumed popcorn, but chances are that the kernels got too close to a fire every now and then and gave the cave men a surprise of their life! The earliest evidence of popcorn as we know it, actually being created was in New Mexico around thirty-six hundred BC.

Fast forward a few thousand years, to the English discovering popcorn after Columbus sailed to America and learned the secret of popping kernels from the Native Americans. Around the same time, Hernando Cortes was learning about the same secret from the Aztecs in Mexico, where popcorn was revered as an important food source and also for its use in ceremonial decorations.

Popcorn was brought by the Native Americans to the first Thanksgiving. Back then, it wasn't eaten like it is today. Instead of separating the kernels from the ear of corn and eating each separately, they would douse the ear in oil and hold it over a fire. Then, after the kernels had popped, they would eat the popcorn from the cob, just as most people eat an ear of corn today. Native Americans would also use popcorn for brewing beer and in soup. The first colonists began using popcorn as a cereal, serving it with milk or cream inside a bowl.

Charles Cretors is the man who created the first popcorn machine on December 2nd, 1885. It all started when he decided to purchase a peanut roaster for his confectionary shop. He wasn't very pleased with the machine's efficiency, so he decided to upgrade the machine by placing a small steam engine inside it! This automated the entire process of roasting peanuts. A traveling salesman named J. M. Savage happened across Cretors' store one day and was amazed when he saw the new machine. He offered to sell the machine to store owners in his sales territory, and Cretors agreed. It wasn't long before he had great success selling his machine and moved to Chicago, where he began to try selling the machine outside of his own shop. While putting it on display, he decided to test the machines limits by roasting more than just peanuts. He soon found that the machine could also pop corn efficiently and modified his machine to roast peanuts and pop corn at the same time.

If you have an electric popcorn machine at home, it is most likely a hot air machine. This type of home machine was not widely available until 1978, when Presto came out with the Popcorn Pumper. Hot air machines have revolutionized popcorn forever because they don't require oil, which reduces the amount of calories and fat created during the process of popping corn. Hot air machines are also a much faster alternative to popping corn in a frying pan and are much less messy than the Cretors popcorn machine!

Home hot air machines didn't become as popular as they could have been, due to the arrival in the mid 1970s of microwave popcorn. Microwave popcorn completely eliminated the need for a dedicated popcorn machine and allows people to make servings of popcorn quickly without having to measure out the amount of kernels. Microwave popcorn is created much faster than any other method of creating popcorn, but it is also unhealthier, deriving more than sixty percent of its calories from fat.

Ways of Cooking Popcorn

$\mathcal{P}$opcorn has been enjoyed by billions of people over the millennia. Many different methods of popping corn have been discovered, but we didn't really know just why popcorn popped, until few centuries back. It's a timeless treat that you can eat or craft with and enjoy, nearly anywhere at any time—if you know just how to pop the kernels.

The key ingredient used to kernel popping is natural ocurring water. There is a small amount inside each kernel, surrounded by soft starch, encased in a hard outer shell that is very difficult to crack open manually. This is made much easier when you heat the kernel up—usually to about four hundred and fifty degrees Fahrenheit! At that temperature, the water inside the kernel turns to steam and creates pressure. This pressure builds until the hard shell of the kernel explodes and the kernel is turned inside out.

The force exerted when a kernel explodes causes it to go all over the place. To keep popcorn from spilling all around your kitchen floor or the ground of your campsite, you have to make sure the kernels are covered. Most methods of creating popcorn cover the kernels or direct their flow in a way that prevents any from being wasted. Now that you know how the process works, let's take a look at some of the different popcorn creation methods.

The first method we are going to discuss is also the oldest—the open fire. Popcorn is a great snack that can be easily made over a campfire. All you need are kernels, a pot, pan, or other cooking device with a long handle, and a way to cover the cooking device you decide to use. Put the cooking container on the fire, make sure it is sitting above the flames, throw the kernels into the container and then cover the top. You should hear the kernels popping after a few minutes and will know it is safe to remove the cover and start eating once the popping has ceased.

The next most common method is the stove top. As civilization and technology progressed, fewer people were living the nomadic lifestyle and sleeping outdoors. The stove replaced the campfire and that made many recipes obsoloete, however the recipe for popcorn hasn't changed much from the campfire setting. All you have to do is put the kernels inside a pan, cover the pan, heat it, and wait for the popping to start and stop. But it is easier to take things a couple steps further when cooking on a stove. Coating the bottom of the pan in cooking oil will give the popcorn a little added flavor. You can also easily melt some butter in the pan, and add whatever seasonings you have on hand. If you want things to be really easy, you can buy prepackaged stove-toppopcorn kits that work by simply turning the stove on and sitting the package onto the burner for a specified period of time.

And now we have finally arrived to the most common method used for making popcorn today—microwaved and popcorn machines! Essentially the same principals—throw the popcorn in, wait, extract, and eat. The only difference between a popcorn machine and microwavable popcorn, is that the latter is prepackaged, like the machine equivalent to the stove-top kit. The only problem with prepackaged popcorn is that it generally comes with artifical flavoring, seasoning and additives, which doesn't leave much room for experimentation. Home popcorn machines simply require you to measure out the amount of kernels you want, easily and safely pop them and then allow you to add the seasonings and flavorings of your choice. And that is exactly what we will be doing in this book.

Sweet Popcorn Recipes

1. Almost Lemon Meringue Popcorn

1/2 cup water
1 cup light corn syrup
2 tbsp lemon zest, freshly grated
1 tbsp lemon juice, freshly squeezed
1/2 cup sugar, granulated
1/4 tsp sea salt
9 cups popcorn, air-popped
1 cup miniature marshmallows
1 tsp sugar, powdered

1. Pour water and corn syrup into small pan over a low heat.
2. Add lemon zest, lemon juice, granulated sugar and salt.
3. Stir continuously until sugar is dissolved.
4. Place the popcorn into a large bowl.
5. Pour liquid over the popcorn and stir well.
6. Spread over waxed paper or onto a non-stick baking sheet, and allow to cool.
7. Pour into a serving bowl, and mix in marshmallows.
8. Dust with powdered sugar and serve.

Servings: 4

Cooking Times

Preparation Time: 10 minutes
Cooking Time: 15 minutes
Inactive Time: 20 minutes
Total Time: 45 minutes

Nutrition Facts

Serving size: 1/4 of a recipe (8.4 ounces).

Amount Per Serving

Calories 474.02
Calories From Fat (2%) 10.77

% Daily Value

Total Fat 1.26g 2%
Saturated Fat 0.14g <1%
Cholesterol 0mg 0%
Sodium 1433.26mg 60%
Potassium 129.16mg 4%
Total Carbohydrates 121.93g 41%
Fiber 3.21g 13%
Sugar 58.74g
Protein 2.9g 6%

Percent daily values based on the Reference Daily Intake (RDI) for a 2000 calorie diet.

 C8 80

2. Baked White Chocolate Popcorn

9 cups popcorn, air-popped
1/2 cup butter, unsalted
1/3 cup brown sugar, packed
1/4 tsp light corn syrup
1/2 tsp sea salt
1/4 tsp baking soda
1 tsp vanilla extract
4 ounces white chocolate chips
cooking spray (as needed)

1. Preheat the oven to 300° F.
2. Lightly coat the sides of a large roasting pan with cooking spray, then add the popcorn.
3. In a small thick bottomed pan over a low heat, melt the butter over a low heat.
4. Add the brown sugar, corn syrup and salt to the pan, then slowly bring the mixture to the boil, stirring constantly
5. Reduce the heat, and simmer for a further 1-2 minutes.
6. Remove pan from heat, then add baking soda and vanilla extract, stirring well.
7. Drizzle this mixture over the popcorn and shake the roasting pan well, ensuring even coverage.
8. Bake the popcorn for 30 minutes, stirring every 10 minutes.
9. Remove popcorn mixture from the oven and sprinkle with chocolate chips.
10. Allow chocolate chips to melt and mixture to cool completely before serving.

Servings: 4

Oven Temperature: 300°F

Cooking Times

Preparation Time: 15 minutes

Cooking Time: 30 minutes
Inactive Time: 15 minutes
Total Time: 1 hour

_____

Nutrition Facts

Serving size: 1/4 of a recipe (3.5 ounces).

_____

Amount Per Serving

Calories 491.72
Calories From Fat (57%) 279.79

_____

% Daily Value

Total Fat 32.6g 50%
Saturated Fat 19.67g 98%
Cholesterol 61.01mg 20%
Sodium 2825.82mg 118%
Potassium 195.42mg 6%
Total Carbohydrates 51.63g 17%
Fiber 4.46g 18%
Sugar 18.19g
Protein 3.96g 8%

_____

Percent daily values based on the Reference Daily Intake (RDI) for a 2000 calorie diet.

☞ ☜

3. Beautiful Butterscotch Popcorn Squares

1/3 cup butter, unsalted
1/2 cup light corn syrup
4 ounces butterscotch chips
1/2 cup peanut butter, crunchy
9 cups popcorn, air-popped

1. Add butter and corn syrup to small pan on a low heat.
2. When butter has melted, gradually add butterscotch chips, stirring continuously.
3. Finally add peanut butter, and keep stirring until melted.
4. Place popcorn in large mixing bowl.
5. Pour mixture over popcorn and stir to cover evenly.
6. Press combined mixture into a non-stick baking dish, and chill for at least an hour.
7. Cut into squares and serve.

Servings: 5

Cooking Times

Preparation Time: 10 minutes
Cooking Time: 15 minutes
Inactive Time: 1 hour
Total Time: 1 hour and 25 minutes

Nutrition Facts

Serving size: 1/5 of a recipe (4 ounces).

Amount Per Serving

Calories 501.92
Calories From Fat (46%) 229.46

% Daily Value

Total Fat 26.78g 41%
Saturated Fat 10.81g 54%
Cholesterol 34.55mg 12%
Sodium 152.13mg 6%
Potassium 218.79mg 6%
Total Carbohydrates 64.07g 21%
Fiber 3.64g 15%
Sugar 11.64g
Protein 8.49g 17%

Percent daily values based on the Reference Daily Intake (RDI) for a 2000 calorie diet.

C8 80

4. Blueberry Butter Popcorn

1/3 cup butter, unsalted
1/4 tsp sea salt
3 tsp sugar, powdered
1/2 tsp blue food coloring
9 cups popcorn, air-popped
1 cup dried blueberries

1. Add butter, salt, sugar and food coloring to small pan on a low heat.
2. Mix popcorn and blueberries in large bowl.
3. Drizzle blue butter mixture over popcorn and stir to cover evenly.
4. Mix well and serve.

Servings: 4

Cooking Times

Preparation Time: 10 minutes
Cooking Time: 10 minutes
Total Time: 20 minutes

Nutrition Facts
Serving size: 1/4 of a recipe (2.8 ounces).

Amount Per Serving

Calories 347.38
Calories From Fat (42%) 146.63

% Daily Value

Total Fat 16.73g 26%
Saturated Fat 9.81g 49%
Cholesterol 40.63mg 14%
Sodium 1375.6mg 57%
Potassium 63.85mg 2%
Total Carbohydrates 49.3g 16%
Fiber 4.7g 19%
Sugar 4.75g
Protein 3.57g 7%

———————————————————————

Percent daily values based on the Reference Daily Intake (RDI) for a 2000 calorie diet.

CB BO

5. Candied Cherry Almond Popcorn

9 cups popcorn, air-popped
1 cup slivered almonds
1/2 cup dried cherries
1/2 cup light corn syrup
3/4 cup water
1 1/2 cup sugar, granulated
1/2 tsp sea salt
2 tbsp butter, unsalted
1 tsp vanilla extract

1. Preheat the oven to 350° F.
2. Lightly coat the sides of a large roasting pan with cooking spray, then add the popcorn, almonds and cherries.
3. Bake for 10 minutes, then turn off the oven, leaving the mixture inside to keep warm.
4. Add the corn syrup, water, sugar and salt to a heavy saucepan and stir over a low heat until dissolved.
5. Continue to heat and stir until the temperature of the liquid reaches 300° F, checking with a candy thermometer.
6. Remove popcorn mixture from oven.
7. Remove liquid from heat and blend in butter and vanilla.
8. Immediately pour over popcorn, and mix well.
9. Allow to cool, and then serve.

Servings: 5

Oven Temperature: 350°F

Cooking Times

Preparation Time: 10 minutes
Cooking Time: 25 minutes
Total Time: 35 minutes

Nutrition Facts

Serving size: 1/5 of a recipe (6.9 ounces).

Amount Per Serving

Calories 646.18
Calories From Fat (26%) 169.93

% Daily Value

Total Fat 20.04g 31%
Saturated Fat 4.11g 21%
Cholesterol 12.21mg 4%
Sodium 2214.68mg 92%
Potassium 248.39mg 7%
Total Carbohydrates 116.31g 39%
Fiber 6.04g 24%
Sugar 70.6g
Protein 8.26g 17%

Percent daily values based on the Reference Daily Intake (RDI) for a 2000 calorie diet.

CB ED

6. Cinnamon S'More Popcorn Trail Mix

7 cups popcorn, air-popped
1 cup Golden Grahams® Cinnamon Toast Crunch
1 cup miniature marshmallows
1/2 cup banana chips
1/2 cup raisins, seedless
1/2 cup cherries, dried
1/3 cup pumpkin seeds, roasted & salted
Add all the ingredients to a serving bowl and mix well.

Servings: 5

Cooking Times

Preparation Time: 5 minutes
Total Time: 5 minutes

Nutrition Facts

Serving size: 1/5 of a recipe (2.3 ounces).

Amount Per Serving

Calories 228.88
Calories From Fat (10%) 23.3

% Daily Value

Total Fat 2.75g 4%
Saturated Fat 1.09g 5%
Cholesterol 0mg 0%
Sodium 168.52mg 7%
Potassium 224.12mg 6%
Total Carbohydrates 51.02g 17%
Fiber 4.24g 17%
Sugar 18.9g
Protein 3.69g 7%

Percent daily values based on the Reference Daily Intake (RDI) for a 2000 calorie diet.

CB ED

7. Coffee Chocolate Liqueur Popcorn—Adults Only!

1 cup chocolate chips, semisweet
4 tsp instant coffee
1 measure Kahlua® or Tia Maria® coffee liqueur
1/4 cup water
9 cups popcorn, air-popped

1. Add chocolate chips, instant coffee, liqueur and water to small pan over a low heat.
2. Stir continuously until chocolate is melted.
3. Place the popcorn into a large bowl.
4. Pour mixture over the popcorn and stir well.
5. Spread over waxed paper or onto a non-stick baking sheet, and allow to set.
6. Break into approx. 2" pieces and serve.

Servings: 10

Cooking Times

Preparation Time: 10 minutes
Cooking Time: 15 minutes
Inactive Time: 30 minutes
Total Time: 55 minutes

Nutrition Facts

Serving size: 1/10 of a recipe (1.2 ounces).

Amount Per Serving

Calories 120.55

Calories From Fat (36%) 43.04

% Daily Value

Total Fat 5.38g 8%
Saturated Fat 3.03g 15%
Cholesterol 0mg 0%
Sodium 3.01mg <1%
Potassium 37.52mg 1%
Total Carbohydrates 18.04g 6%
Fiber 2.03g 8%
Sugar 1.68g
Protein 1.68g 3%

Percent daily values based on the Reference Daily Intake (RDI) for a 2000 calorie diet.

C8 80

8. Double Peanut Popcorn

1/4 cup butter, unsalted
1/2 cup peanut butter, crunchy
1 tsp sugar, brown
9 cups popcorn, air-popped
3/4 cup peanuts, roasted without salt

1. Add butter to small pan on a low heat.
2. When butter has melted, add peanut butter and sugar, stir until melted.
3. Mix popcorn and peanuts together in a large bowl.
4. Pour butter mixture over the popcorn, stir well and serve.

Servings: 4

Cooking Times

Preparation Time: 10 minutes
Cooking Time: 10 minutes
Total Time: 20 minutes

Nutrition Facts

Serving size: 1/4 of a recipe (3.3 ounces).

Amount Per Serving

Calories 525.51
Calories From Fat (68%) 357.64

% Daily Value

Total Fat 42.17g 65%
Saturated Fat 12.67g 63%
Cholesterol 30.5mg 10%
Sodium 152.99mg 6%
Potassium 453.58mg 13%
Total Carbohydrates 27.35g 9%
Fiber 6.74g 27%
Sugar 5.39g
Protein 17.03g 34%

Percent daily values based on the Reference Daily Intake (RDI) for a 2000 calorie diet.

CB ED

2 tbsp orange zest, freshly grated
1 tsp dill weed, fresh
9 cups popcorn, air-popped
1 tbsp sugar, powdered

1. In a small bowl, mix the orange zest and dill weed.
2. Leave for 30 minutes for flavors to infuse.
3. Add the popcorn to a large serving bowl, and mix in the lemon and dill weed.
4. Sprinkle with sugar and serve.

Servings: 3

Cooking Times

Preparation Time: 10 minutes
Inactive Time: 30 minutes
Total Time: 40 minutes

Nutrition Facts

Serving size: 1/3 of a recipe (1.1 ounces).

Amount Per Serving

Calories 104.89
Calories From Fat (9%) 9.19

% Daily Value

Total Fat 0.14g <1%
Cholesterol 0mg 0%
Sodium 2.12mg <1%
Potassium 87.94mg 3%
Total Carbohydrates 21.78g 7%
Fiber 3.91g 16%
Sugar 2.25g
Protein 3.17g 6%

Percent daily values based on the Reference Daily Intake (RDI) for a 2000 calorie diet.

CB BO

10. Happy Holidays Popcorn

1/4 cup butter, unsalted
2 tbs sugar, powdered
3/4 tsp ground cinnamon
3/4 tsp ground nutmeg
9 cups popcorn, air-popped
1 tsp candy sprinkles

1. Add butter to small pan on a low heat.
2. When butter has melted, stir in sugar, cinnamon and nutmeg.
3. Place the popcorn in a large bowl.
4. Pour butter mixture over the popcorn and stir well.
5. Mix in candy sprinkles and serve immediately.

Servings: 3

Cooking Times

Preparation Time: 10 minutes

Cooking Time: 10 minutes

Total Time: 20 minutes

Nutrition Facts

Serving size: 1/3 of a recipe (1.8 ounces).

Amount Per Serving

Calories 256.25
Calories From Fat (57%) 146.04

% Daily Value

Total Fat 16.64g 26%
Saturated Fat 10g 50%
Cholesterol 40.67mg 14%
Sodium 4.26mg <1%
Potassium 88.33mg 3%
Total Carbohydrates 25.32g 8%
Fiber 3.94g 16%
Sugar 5.61g
Protein 3.32g 7%

Percent daily values based on the Reference Daily Intake (RDI) for a 2000 calorie diet.

CR 80

11. Lavender Lime Popcorn

1/3 cup butter, unsalted
1/4 tsp sea salt
1 tbsp sugar, powdered
1 tbsp lime zest
8 drops purple food coloring
1/2 tsp lavender extract
9 cups popcorn, air-popped

1. Add butter, salt, sugar, lime zest and food coloring to small pan on a low heat.
2. Stir until butter is melted, then remove from heat and add lavender extract.
3. Place popcorn in large mixing bowl.
4. Drizzle purple butter mixture over popcorn and stir to cover evenly.
5. Mix well and serve.

Servings: 4

Cooking Times

Preparation Time: 10 minutes
Cooking Time: 10 minutes
Total Time: 20 minutes

Nutrition Facts

Serving size: 1/4 of a recipe (1.5 ounces).

Amount Per Serving

Calories 217.71
Calories From Fat (65%) 142.53

% Daily Value

Total Fat 16.24g 25%
Saturated Fat 9.81g 49%
Cholesterol 40.63mg 14%
Sodium 1370.69mg 57%
Potassium 66.96mg 2%
Total Carbohydrates 16.5g 6%
Fiber 2.86g 11%
Sugar 1.76g
Protein 2.6g 5%

Percent daily values based on the Reference Daily Intake (RDI) for a 2000 calorie diet.

CB ED

12. Pistachio Praline Popcorn

1/4 cupbutter, unsalted
1/2 cup brown sugar, packed
1 tsp cinnamon, ground
9 cups popcorn, air-popped
2/3 cup shelled pistachio nuts, roasted without salt

1. Add butter to small pan on a low heat.
2. When butter has melted, add sugar and cinnamon, stir until sugar has dissolved.
3. Mix popcorn and together in a large bowl.
4. Pour butter mixture over the popcorn and stir well.
5. Spread over waxed paper or onto a non-stick baking sheet, and allow to cool before serving.

Servings: 4

Cooking Times

Preparation Time: 10 minutes
Cooking Time: 10 minutes
Total Time: 20 minutes

Nutrition Facts

Serving size: 1/4 of a recipe (2.9 ounces).

Amount Per Serving

Calories 393.78
Calories From Fat (47%) 184.96

% Daily Value

Total Fat 21.53g 33%
Saturated Fat 8.51g 43%
Cholesterol 30.5mg 10%
Sodium 12mg <1%
Potassium 308.54mg 9%
Total Carbohydrates 47.56g 16%
Fiber 4.99g 20%
Sugar 28.45g
Protein 6.81g 14%

Percent daily values based on the Reference Daily Intake (RDI) for a 2000 calorie diet.

Cʒ ঙ

2 cups chocolate chips, semisweet
1/4 cup butter, unsalted
2 tbsp shortening
2 cups miniature marshmallows
1 cup peanuts, roasted, without salt
7 cups popcorn, air-popped
1/2 cup raisins, seedless

1. Add chocolate chips, butter and shortening to small pan over a low heat.
2. Stir continuously until chocolate is melted.
3. Add marshmallows, stirring until they begin to melt, then immediately remove pan from heat.
4. Place the peanuts, popcorn and raisins into a mixing bowl and stir.
5. Pour chocolate mixture over the popcorn and stir well.
6. Press combined mixture into a non-stick baking dish, and chill for at least an hour.
7. Cut into squares and then serve.

Servings: 10

Cooking Times

Preparation Time: 10 minutes
Cooking Time: 15 minutes
Inactive Time: 1 hour
Total Time: 1 hour and 25 minutes

Nutrition Facts

Serving size: 1/10 of a recipe (2.5 ounces).

Amount Per Serving

Calories 352.74
Calories From Fat (57%) 201.27

% Daily Value

Total Fat 24.09g 37%
Saturated Fat 10.86g 54%
Cholesterol 13.63mg 5%
Sodium 7.59mg <1%
Potassium 172.35mg 5%
Total Carbohydrates 35.85g 12%
Fiber 4.02g 16%
Sugar 6.29g
Protein 5.97g 12%

Percent daily values based on the Reference Daily Intake (RDI) for a 2000 calorie diet.

 CB ⊗O

14. Rum 'n' Root Beer Popcorn Balls—Adults Only!

3/4 cup butter, unsalted
1/2 cup brown sugar, packed
1/2 tsp sea salt
1 tsp root beer extract
1 jigger Captain Morgan® Original Spiced Rum
1 cup water
1/2 cup light corn syrup
9 cups popcorn, air-popped
1/2 cup peanuts, roasted, without salt
cooking spray (as needed)

1. In a small thick bottomed pan, melt the butter over a low heat.
2. Add the brown sugar, salt, root beer extract, rum, water and corn syrup to the pan, stirring constantly.
3. Continue to heat and stir until the temperature reaches 240º F, checking with a candy thermometer.
4. Add popcorn and peanuts to a large bowl and mix well.
5. Drizzle mixture over the popcorn and stir well, ensuring even coverage.
6. To avoid burning your hands, allow coated popcorn to cool for 10 minutes.
7. Roll mixture into balls, chill for 15 minutes and then serve.

Tip

Grease your hands with a little cooking spray before rolling each ball.

Servings: 10

Cooking Times

Preparation Time: 20 minutes
Cooking Time: 15 minutes
Inactive Time: 25 minutes
Total Time: 1 hour

Nutrition Facts

Serving size: 1/10 of a recipe (1.8 ounces).

Amount Per Serving

Calories 246.02
Calories From Fat (62%) 152.94

% Daily Value

Total Fat 17.55g 27%
Saturated Fat 9.25g 46%
Cholesterol 36.6mg 12%
Sodium 1099.86mg 46%
Potassium 88.47mg 3%
Total Carbohydrates 18.45g 6%
Fiber 1.57g 6%
Sugar 11.15g
Protein 2.91g 6%

Percent daily values based on the Reference Daily Intake (RDI) for a 2000 calorie diet.

CG 80

15. Sticky Strawberry Popcorn Balls

9 cups popcorn, air-popped
3/4 cup butter, unsalted
1/2 cup brown sugar, packed
1 3 oz pack Jell-O® Strawberry Gelatin Dessert
3 tbs water
1 tbsp light corn syrup
cooking spray (as needed)

1. Preheat the oven to 300º F.
2. Lightly coat the sides of a large roasting pan with cooking spray, then add the popcorn.
3. In a small thick bottomed pan over a low heat, melt the butter over a low heat.
4. Add the brown sugar, Jell-O®, water and corn syrup to the pan, stirring constantly.
5. Continue to heat and stir until the temperature of the liquid reaches 270º F, checking with a candy thermometer.
6. Drizzle this mixture over the popcorn and shake the roasting pan well, ensuring even coverage.
7. Bake the popcorn for 10 minutes, stirring after 5 minutes.
8. Remove popcorn mixture from the oven and allow to cool to room temperature.
9. Roll mixture into balls, chill for 15 minutes then serve.

Tip

Keep a bowl of cold water close by, making sure to dip your hands into it before rolling each ball.

Servings: 10

Oven Temperature: 300°F

Cooking Times

Preparation Time: 25 minutes
Cooking Time: 30 minutes
Inactive Time: 15 minutes
Total Time: 1 hour and 10 minutes

Nutrition Facts

Serving size: 1/10 of a recipe (1.4 ounces).

Amount Per Serving

Calories 202.22
Calories From Fat (55%) 111.01

% Daily Value

Total Fat 14.2g 22%
Saturated Fat 8.79g 44%
Cholesterol 36.6mg 12%
Sodium 15.07mg <1%
Potassium 44.24mg 1%
Total Carbohydrates 18.81g 6%
Fiber 1.04g 4%
Sugar 12.81g
Protein 1.29g 3%

Percent daily values based on the Reference Daily Intake (RDI) for a 2000 calorie diet.

ଓଃ ଶ୦

Savory Popcorn Recipes

16. Caribbean Sunset Layered Popcorn

1 tsp jerk seasoning
1/4 tsp ground allspice
1 tsp curry powder
1/4 tsp cayenne pepper
1/4 tsp sea salt
1 tsp lemon zest
9 cups popcorn, air-popped
1/4 cup banana chips, dried
cooking spray, as needed

1. In a small bowl, blend the jerk seasoning, allspice, curry powder, cayenne, salt and lemon zest.
2. Spray the insides of a serving bowl with cooking spray.
3. Add a layer of approx. 2 cups popcorn to the bowl.
4. Sprinkle a layer of the seasoning blend on top (approx 1/3 of the mixture)
5. Add another layer of popcorn, and repeat until all ingredients have been used.
6. Top with banana chips.
7. Do not mix before serving!

Servings: 3

Cooking Times

Preparation Time: 10 minutes
Total Time: 10 minutes

Nutrition Facts

Serving size: 1/3 of a recipe (2.2 ounces).

Amount Per Serving

Calories 181.59
Calories From Fat (19%) 35.16

% Daily Value

Total Fat 3.84g 6%
Saturated Fat 0.87g 4%
Cholesterol 0mg 0%
Sodium 607.17 mg 253%
Potassium 107.65mg 3%
Total Carbohydrates 31.44g 10%
Fiber 5.63g 23%
Sugar 1.11g
Protein 4.88g 10%

Percent daily values based on the Reference Daily Intake (RDI) for a 2000 calorie diet.

ଔ ଓ

17. Five Spice Peanut Popcorn

9 cups popcorn, air-popped
1 cup roasted peanuts, without salt
1 tbsp soy sauce
1/4 cup peanut oil
1/2 tsp ground ginger
1/4 tsp sea salt
1/4 tsp cayenne pepper
1 tsp five spice powder
1 tsp fresh garlic, minced
cooking spray, as needed

1. Preheat the oven to 330° F.
2. Lightly coat the sides of a large roasting pan with cooking spray.
3. Add the popcorn and peanuts to the pan and mix well.
4. In a small bowl combine the soy sauce, oil, ginger, salt, cayenne, five spice, and garlic powder.
5. Drizzle over popcorn mixture.
6. Bake for 10 minutes, stirring once.
7. Serve hot or cold.

Servings: 4

Oven Temperature: 330°F

Cooking Times

Preparation Time: 10 minutes
Cooking Time: 15 minutes
Total Time: 25 minutes

Nutrition Facts

Serving size: 1/4 of a recipe (2.5 ounces).

Amount Per Serving

Calories 391.88
Calories From Fat (68%) 266.46

% Daily Value

Total Fat 31.04g 48%
Saturated Fat 4.7g 24%
Cholesterol 0mg 0%
Sodium 1415.18mg 59%
Potassium 301.37mg 9%
Total Carbohydrates 21.82g 7%
Fiber 5.18g 21%
Sugar 1.59g
Protein 11.36g 23%

Percent daily values based on the Reference Daily Intake (RDI) for a 2000 calorie diet.

CR ⅋ EO

18. Gorgeous Greek Popcorn

1/2 cup feta cheese, crumbled
1/2 cup kasseri cheese, grated
1 tsp oregano, chopped fresh
2 tsp basil, chopped fresh
1/4 tsp sea salt
9 cups popcorn, air-popped

1. In a small bowl, combine the cheeses, oregano, basil and salt.
2. Place the popcorn in a large bowl.
3. Sprinkle with the cheese and herb mixture, and toss—then serve.

Servings: 3

Cooking Times

Preparation Time: 10 minutes
Total Time: 10 minutes

Nutrition Facts

Serving size: 1/3 of a recipe (2.7 ounces).

Amount Per Serving

Calories 248.79
Calories From Fat (45%) 111.07

% Daily Value

Total Fat 12.66g 19%
Saturated Fat 7.79g 39%
Cholesterol 42.49mg 14%
Sodium 2145.92mg 89%
Potassium 119.52mg 3%
Total Carbohydrates 21.84g 7%
Fiber 3.76g 15%
Sugar 1.53g
Protein 12.78g 26%

Percent daily values based on the Reference Daily Intake (RDI) for a 2000 calorie diet.

CS ∞

19. Hazelnut Herb Popcorn

1/4 cup butter, unsalted
1/2 tbsp rosemary, finely chopped fresh
1 tsp sea salt
1/2 tsp chervil, dried
9 cups popcorn, air-popped
3/4 cup hazelnuts, roasted without salt
1 tbsp basil, chopped fresh

1. Add butter to small pan on a low heat.
2. When butter has melted, stir in rosemary, chervil and salt.
3. Place the popcorn, hazelnuts and basil into a large bowl and mix.
4. Pour butter mixture over the popcorn, stir well and serve.

Servings: 3

Cooking Times

Preparation Time: 10 minutes
Cooking Time: 10 minutes
Total Time: 20 minutes

Nutrition Facts

Serving size: 1/3 of a recipe (3.9 ounces).

Amount Per Serving

Calories 616.89
Calories From Fat (72%) 445.17

% Daily Value

Total Fat 52.32g 80%
Saturated Fat 12.42g 62%
Cholesterol 40.67mg 14%
Sodium 294.86mg 12%
Potassium 520.82mg 15%
Total Carbohydrates 32.02g 11%
Fiber 9.36g 37%
Sugar 3g
Protein 12.33g 25%

Percent daily values based on the Reference Daily Intake (RDI) for a 2000 calorie diet.

20. Hickory Jack Popcorn

1/3 cup butter, unsalted
1/2 tsp hickory-smoked salt
1/4 cup bacon bits, meatless
9 cups popcorn, air-popped
1/2 cup grated Monterey Jack cheese

1. Add butter to small pan on a low heat.
2. When butter has melted, stir in hickory-smoked salt and bacon bits.
3. Place popcorn into a mixing bowl.
4. Pour melted butter mixture over popcorn and shake well to coat.
5. Sprinkle with grated cheese and serve.

Servings: 3

Cooking Times

Preparation Time: 15 minutes
Cooking Time: 10 minutes
Total Time: 25 minutes

Nutrition Facts

Serving size: 1/3 of a recipe (2.8 ounces).

Amount Per Serving

Calories 388.9
Calories From Fat (67%) 260.66

% Daily Value

Total Fat 29.65g 46%
Saturated Fat 17.05g 85%
Cholesterol 70.94mg 24%
Sodium 612.55mg 26%
Potassium 113.8mg 3%
Total Carbohydrates 21.68g 7%
Fiber 4.6g 18%
Sugar 0.32g
Protein 10.92g 22%

Percent daily values based on the Reference Daily Intake (RDI) for a 2000 calorie diet.

ᙆ ᙇ

1/4 cup butter, unsalted
1 tbsp yellow mustard, prepared
1 tsp chili powder
1/4 tsp ground cumin
1/4 tsp sea salt
9 cups popcorn, air-popped

1. Add butter to small pan on a low heat.
2. When butter has melted, stir in mustard, chili powder, cumin and salt.
3. Place the popcorn in a large bowl.
4. Pour mustard mixture over the popcorn and stir well, then serve.

Servings: 3

Cooking Times

Preparation Time: 10 minutes
Cooking Time: 10 minutes
Total Time: 20 minutes

Nutrition Facts

Serving size: 1/3 of a recipe (1.8 ounces).

Amount Per Serving

Calories 240.52
Calories From Fat (62%) 148.39

% Daily Value

Total Fat 16.93g 26%
Saturated Fat 9.89g 49%
Cholesterol 40.67mg 14%
Sodium 1900.85mg 79%
Potassium 111.37mg 3%
Total Carbohydrates 20.31g 7%
Fiber 4.1g 16%
Sugar 0.33g
Protein 3.77g 8%

Percent daily values based on the Reference Daily Intake (RDI) for a 2000 calorie diet.

 CG 80

22. Party Pizza Popcorn

2 tbsp grated Parmesan cheese
1/2 tsp garlic powder
1 tsp Italian seasoning
1/2 tsp paprika
1/4 tsp sea salt
1/4 tsp black pepper, freshly ground
9 cups popcorn, air-popped

1. Add all ingredients, except popcorn, to your blender or food processor and whiz for 2-3 minutes.
2. Place the popcorn in a large bowl.
3. Sprinkle with the cheese mixture, and toss—then serve.

Servings: 3

Cooking Times

Preparation Time: 15 minutes
Total Time: 15 minutes

_____

Nutrition Facts

Serving size: 1/3 of a recipe (1.1 ounces).

_____

Amount Per Serving

Calories 116.79
Calories From Fat (17%) 19.39

_____

% Daily Value

Total Fat 2.25g 3%
Saturated Fat 0.73g 4%
Cholesterol 2.93mg <1%
Sodium 1876.32mg 78%
Potassium 100.36mg 3%
Total Carbohydrates 20.56g 7%
Fiber 3.89g 16%
Sugar 0.29g
Protein 4.7g 9%

Percent daily values based on the Reference Daily Intake (RDI) for a 2000 calorie diet.

⋐ ⋑

23. Perfect PopChex

1/3 cup butter, unsalted
1 tsp soy sauce
1 dash hot sauce
9 cups popcorn, air-popped
2 cups Chex Mix®

1. Add butter to small pan on a low heat.
2. When butter has melted, add soya sauce and hot sauce.
3. Add the popcorn and Chex Mix® to a large bowl.
4. Stir well, then serve.

Servings: 4

Cooking Times

Preparation Time: 10 minutes
Cooking Time: 10 minutes
Total Time: 20 minutes

Nutrition Facts

Serving size: 1/4 of a recipe (1.9 ounces).

Amount Per Serving

Calories 265.99
Calories From Fat (58%) 154.37

% Daily Value

Total Fat 17.56g 27%
Saturated Fat 10.02g 50%
Cholesterol 40.63mg 14%
Sodium 160.65mg 7%
Potassium 94.36mg 3%
Total Carbohydrates 24.75g 8%
Fiber 3.17g 13%
Sugar 0.88g
Protein 3.81g 8%

Percent daily values based on the Reference Daily Intake (RDI) for a 2000 calorie diet.

ಐ ಏ

1/4 cup butter, unsalted
1 tsp Italian seasoning
1/2 tsp garlic salt
9 cups popcorn, air-popped
1/2 cup Romano cheese

1. Add butter to small pan on a low heat.
2. When butter has melted, stir in Italian seasoning and garlic salt.
3. Pour butter mixture over the popcorn and stir well.
4. Sprinkle with cheese and toss—then serve.

Servings: 4

Cooking Times

Preparation Time: 10 minutes
Cooking Time: 10 minutes
Total Time: 20 minutes

Nutrition Facts

Serving size: 1/4 of a recipe (3.2 ounces).

Amount Per Serving

Calories 392.06
Calories From Fat (62%) 242.55

% Daily Value

Total Fat 27.62g 42%
Saturated Fat 17.09g 85%
Cholesterol 89.47mg 30%
Sodium 939.77mg 39%
Potassium 111.39mg 3%
Total Carbohydrates 16.39g 5%
Fiber 2.79g 11%
Sugar 0.58g
Protein 20.5g 41%

Percent daily values based on the Reference Daily Intake (RDI) for a 2000 calorie diet.

 C3 80

25. Pumpkin Chip Popcorn

1/4 cup butter, unsalted
1 tbsp taco sauce
1 tsp taco seasoning mix
7 cups popcorn, air-popped
1 cup pumpkin seeds, roasted & salted
1 cup corn chips

1. Preheat oven to 320° F.
2. Add butter to small pan on a low heat.
3. When butter has melted, stir in taco sauce and taco seasoning.
4. Place popcorn, pumpkin seeds and corn chips in a roasting pan.
5. Pour butter mixture over the contents of the roasting pan and mix well.
6. Bake for 12 minutes, stirring once.
7. Mix well and serve.

Servings: 4

Oven Temperature: 320°F

Cooking Times

Preparation Time: 10 minutes
Cooking Time: 12 minutes
Total Time: 22 minutes

Nutrition Facts

Serving size: 1/4 of a recipe (2 ounces).

Amount Per Serving

Calories 266.38
Calories From Fat (56%) 150.41

% Daily Value

Total Fat 17.28g 27%
Saturated Fat 8.21g 41%
Cholesterol 30.5mg 10%
Sodium 490.58mg 20%
Potassium 206.07mg 6%
Total Carbohydrates 24.45g 8%
Fiber 5.39g 22%
Sugar 0.46g
Protein 5.4g 11%

Percent daily values based on the Reference Daily Intake (RDI) for a 2000 calorie diet.

CS 80

26. Shoestring Pecan Popcorn

1/4 cup butter, unsalted
1 tsp dill weed, dried
1 tsp lemon pepper
1/2 tsp garlic powder
1/2 tsp onion powder
1/4 tsp sea salt
1 tsp Worcestershire sauce
9 cups popcorn, air-popped
1/2 cup pecans, chopped
2 cups shoestring potato snack sticks

1. Preheat oven to 320° F.
2. Add butter to small pan on a low heat.
3. When butter has melted, stir in dill weed, lemon pepper, garlic powder, onion powder, salt and Worcestershire sauce.
4. Arrange the popcorn, pecans and potato sticks evenly on a large roasting pan.
5. Drizzle with butter and herb mixture and stir well.
6. Bake in oven for 10 minutes, stirring once.
7. Serve warm.

Servings: 4

Oven Temperature: 320°F

Cooking Times

Preparation Time: 10 minutes
Cooking Time: 10 minutes
Total Time: 20 minutes

Nutrition Facts

Serving size: 1/4 of a recipe (2.3 ounces).

Amount Per Serving

Calories 347.43
Calories From Fat (67%) 232.04

% Daily Value

Total Fat 27.11g 42%
Saturated Fat 9.49g 47%
Cholesterol 30.5mg 10%
Sodium 1472.95mg 61%
Potassium 319.68mg 9%
Total Carbohydrates 24.98g 8%
Fiber 4.6g 18%
Sugar 0.89g
Protein 4.88g 10%

Percent daily values based on the Reference Daily Intake (RDI) for a 2000 calorie diet.

 C8 80

27. Smoked Garlic Popcorn

3 tbsp grated Parmesan cheese
1 garlic clove, minced
1/2 tsp smoked garlic powder
1/2 tsp paprika
1/2 tsp sea salt
9 cups popcorn, air-popped

1. In a small bowl, combine the Parmesan and fresh garlic.
2. Add the garlic powder, paprika and salt and mix well.
3. Place the popcorn in a large bowl.
4. Sprinkle with Parmesan garlic mixture, and toss—then serve.

Servings: 3

Cooking Times

Preparation Time: 10 minutes
Total Time: 10 minutes

Nutrition Facts

Serving size: 1/3 of a recipe (1.3 ounces).

Amount Per Serving

Calories 131.06
Calories From Fat (19%) 24.61

% Daily Value

Total Fat 2.82g 4%
Saturated Fat 1.01g 5%
Cholesterol 4.4mg 1%
Sodium 1724.75mg 72%
Potassium 110.29mg 3%
Total Carbohydrates 21.79g 7%
Fiber 3.97g 16%
Sugar 0.33g
Protein 5.56g 11%

Percent daily values based on the Reference Daily Intake (RDI) for a 2000 calorie diet.

છ ૪ઝ

28. Super Simple Savory Popcorn

1/4 cup butter, unsalted
9 cups popcorn, freshly air-popped and still warm
1 1/2 tsp onion powder
1 1/2 tsp garlic powder
1 tsp sea salt
1/3 tsp black pepper, freshly ground

1. Add butter to small pan on a low heat.
2. When butter has melted, stir in salt, onion powder and garlic powder.
3. Place the popcorn in a large bowl.
4. Pour butter mixture over the popcorn and stir well.
5. Sprinkle with black pepper and serve.

Servings: 3

Cooking Times

Preparation Time: 10 minutes
Cooking Time: 10 minutes
Total Time: 20 minutes

Nutrition Facts

Serving size: 1/3 of a recipe (2 ounces).

Amount Per Serving

Calories 259.6
Calories From Fat (57%) 149.11

% Daily Value

Total Fat 16.94g 26%
Saturated Fat 9.86g 49%
Cholesterol 40.67mg 14%
Sodium 7296.52mg 304%
Potassium 116.91mg 3%
Total Carbohydrates 24.13g 8%
Fiber 4.34g 17%
Sugar 0.34g
Protein 4.15g 8%

Percent daily values based on the Reference Daily Intake (RDI) for a 2000 calorie diet.

CB BO

29. Warm Nacho Popcorn

1/4 cup butter, unsalted
1 tsp paprika
1/2 tsp crushed red pepper flakes
1/2 tsp ground cumin
9 cups popcorn, freshly air-popped and still warm
1/2 cup grated Parmesan cheese

1. Add butter to small pan on a low heat.
2. When butter has melted, stir in pepper flakes, cumin and half of the paprika..
3. Place the still warm popcorn in a large bowl.
4. Pour butter mixture over the popcorn and stir well.
5. Sprinkle with Parmesan and toss.
6. Dust with the rest of the paprika—then serve.

Servings: 3

Cooking Times

Preparation Time: 10 minutes
Cooking Time: 10 minutes
Total Time: 20 minutes

Nutrition Facts

Serving size: 1/3 of a recipe (2.1 ounces).

Amount Per Serving

Calories 303.82
Calories From Fat (62%) 187.37

% Daily Value

Total Fat 21.38g 33%
Saturated Fat 12.76g 64%
Cholesterol 55.34mg 18%
Sodium 259.94mg 11%
Potassium 128.07mg 4%
Total Carbohydrates 19.95g 7%
Fiber 3.78g 15%
Sugar 0.46g
Protein 9.85g 20%

Percent daily values based on the Reference Daily Intake (RDI) for a 2000 calorie diet.

CB BO

30. *Wild Wasabi Popcorn*

1 sheet sushi nori seaweed, dried
1/2 tsp sea salt, fine
1/2 tsp wasabi powder
9 cups popcorn, freshly air-popped and still warm

1. Cut the seaweed into thin strips, approx 1/4" wide, with sharp kitchen scissors.
2. Combine the salt and wasabi powder in a small bowl.
3. Place the warm popcorn in a large bowl, and mix in seaweed.
4. Sprinkle with the wasabi salt, and toss—then serve.

Servings: 3

Cooking Times

Preparation Time: 10 minutes
Total Time: 10 minutes

Nutrition Facts

Serving size: 1/3 of a recipe (2.5 ounces).

Amount Per Serving

Calories 223.7
Calories From Fat (17%) 38.59

% Daily Value

Total Fat 4.52g 7%
Saturated Fat 1.14g 6%
Cholesterol 0mg 0%
Sodium 4045.89mg 169%
Potassium 596.59mg 17%
Total Carbohydrates 31.04g 10%
Fiber 5.46g 22%
Sugar 1.4g
Protein 25.1g 50%

Percent daily values based on the Reference Daily Intake (RDI) for a 2000 calorie diet.

CB BD

Harder to Find Ingredients

*M*ost of the ingredients for these recipes can be found at your local grocery store or deli, but if you get stuck, then the slightly more unusual ones can also bought online via this special page on my website

greengourmetbooks.com/ing

How to Get 12 More Perfect Popcorn Recipes

I would love to add another 12 delicious recipes to your collection, as my gift to you.

All you need to do is pop over to my website and sign up for my free newsletter.

greengourmetbooks.com/free

I regularly update my blog with free recipes that you can download, print and rate.
If you follow me on Twitter I'll tweet whenever I've posted a new recipe.
If you 'like' my Facebook page you'll be notified of free Kindle download book days.

I look forward to connecting with you!

Lori

www.greengourmetbooks.com

www.facebook.com/GreenGourmetBooks

@lorijanestewart

http://feeds.feedburner.com/TheGreenGourmet

Other Books You May Enjoy

'. . . finally understand why us Brits love a proper cuppa . . .'—**Geoff Wells** *****

'. . . a splendid analysis of tea and a jolly good read . . .'—**BookishFriend** *****

'. . . a very well researched book that covers a wealth of information on all aspects of tea . . .'—**Syed S. Ahmed** *****

greengourmetbooks.com/tea

'. . . the last diet you'll ever need to follow . . .'—**Sue Walker** *****

'. . . a power house of information . . .'—**C. Vencato** *****

'. . . a perfect combination between a guide and a cookbook . . . .'—**Chris Stomper** *****

'. . . get this book if you'd like to lose weight naturally and be healthy at the same time . . . .'—**Paul** *****

greengourmetbooks.com/diet

'. . . The perfect pocket meatloaf collection . . . another great cookbook by Lori . . .'—**Grace Darby** *****

'. . . Wake up your meatloaf recipes! . . . this book is a keeper . . . .'—**B. Haywood** *****

'. . . thank you Lori for renewing my love of meatloaf . . .'—**Kat** *****

greengourmetbooks.com/meat